African Culture

Catherine Chambers

Raintree

www.raintreepublishers.co.uk
Visit our website to find out more information about Raintree books.

To order:
☎ Phone 0845 6044371
🖨 Fax +44 (0) 1865 312263
✉ Email myorders@raintreepublishers.co.uk

Customers from outside the UK please telephone +44 1865 312262

Raintree is an imprint of Capstone Global Library Limited, a company incorporated in England and Wales having its registered office at 7 Pilgrim Street, London, EC4V 6LB – Registered company number: 6695582

Text © Capstone Global Library Limited 2013
First published in hardback in 2013
Paperback edition first published in 2014
The moral rights of the proprietor have been asserted.

Edited by Charlotte Guillain, Abby Colich, and Vaarunika Dharmapala
Designed by Steve Mead
Original illustrations © Capstone Global Library Ltd 2013
Illustrations by Oxford Designers & Illustrators
Picture research by Ruth Blair
Originated by Capstone Global Library Ltd
Printed and bound in China by Leo Paper Products Ltd

ISBN 978 1 406 24172 3 (hardback)
16 15 14 13 12
10 9 8 7 6 5 4 3 2 1

ISBN 978 1 406 24180 8 (paperback)
17 16 15 14 13
10 9 8 7 6 5 4 3 2 1

British Library Cataloguing in Publication Data
Chambers, Catherine.
African culture. -- (Global cultures)
306'.096-dc23
A full catalogue record for this book is available from the British Library.

Acknowledgements
We would like to thank the following for permission to reproduce photographs: Alamy pp. 5 (© Visions of America, LLC), 6 (© LatitudeStock), 12 (© Picture Contact BV), 13 (© John Warburton-Lee Photography), 14 (© Tom Gilks), 16 (© FORGET Patrick/sagaphoto.com), 27 (© Sabena Jane Blackbird); Corbis pp. 9 (© Antonio Silva/EPA), 15 (© Dai Kurokawa/EPA), 19 (© Patrick Durand/Sygma), 23 (© Bob Krist), 31 (© Gavin Hellier/JAI), 37 (© Ann Johansson), 38 (© David Atlas/Retna Ltd), 41 (© Andrew McConnell/Robert Harding World Imagery); Getty Images pp. 33 (Roberta Parkin/Redferns), 34 (Volkmar K. Wentzel/National Geographic), 39 (Denny Allen); PA Photos p. 35 (AP); Photolibrary pp. 24 (Sylvain Cordier), 26 (Mark Shenley/Still Pictures); © Photoshot pp. 10, 17; Photoshot pp. 11 (© World Pictures), 18 (© NHPA), 21 (© africanpictures.net), 25 (© Eye Ubiquitous), 28 (© Biosphoto), 29 (© UPPA), 30 (© Anka Agency), 32 (© WpN); Shutterstock pp. 36 (© mythja), 43 top left (© Trevor Kittelty), 43 bottom left (© Alex Bonney), 43 bottom right (© Paul Gibbings), 43 top right (© Guido Vrola), design features (© sootra).

Cover photograph of a smiling African girl reproduced with permission of Corbis (© Theo Allofs). Cover design feature of a colourful textile reproduced with permission of Shutterstock (© sootra).

Every effort has been made to contact copyright holders of any material reproduced in this book. Any omissions will be rectified in subsequent printings if notice is given to the publisher.

A Masai herdsman in East Africa blends old culture with new. He is wearing traditional clothing as he chats on a mobile phone.

FAMILY AND COMMUNITY

African culture begins with how people live together. In many families, the parents, children, grandparents, aunts, and uncles might all live as neighbours, or even together. This is called an "extended family".

These family homes with baked clay walls are in the ancient city of Zaria, in Nigeria.

Living together

The family often lives in a compound. This is a **homestead**, sometimes surrounded by **wattle** fences or brick walls. The extended family makes it easier for adults to work and raise children. It is harder to keep this culture in modern cities where many people live in high-rise flats and cramped **shanty towns**. Some families now prefer to live in smaller groups.

Knowing your place

Each person knows their roles and duties. This is especially true in communities that are organized into traditional **age grades**. Each age grade marks a life stage and lasts from 8 to 15 years. This is very different from school grades that last for just a year. Everyone is given responsibilities according to their grade. Age grade systems are used mainly in East Africa but also in some West African societies, such as the Bambara and Igbo. Age grades and their rules are not as strict as they once were.

YOUNG PEOPLE

Among some peoples, boys and men and occasionally girls move through their grades together in a group called an **age set**. Age sets last for life and are often given names such as "Leopard" or "Thunder". In Kenya and Tanzania, Masai boys move up to the *moran* warrior life stage in their teenage years. Here, they learn cattle-keeping skills and Masai **traditions**.

Clans and kinship

There is a strong culture of **kinship** across Africa. It often begins with the **clan**, which is a group of families or villages that share a common language and culture. Each clan or clan group might be led by a committee of senior men called **elders**. Elders help sort out family quarrels and land disputes.

Traditional kings and modern nations

Hundreds of years ago, some clans were brought together under kings and emperors. Today, people still honour these traditional rulers. There are many, from the *Oba* (King) of the Yoruba people in Nigeria, to the *Kabaka* (King) of the Baganda in Uganda.

Kings wear or carry **symbols** of power on ceremonial occasions. These can include ornate fly-whisks and grand parasols. However, today's kings have little power.

Africa has a mixture of old and new political systems. People might keep to tradition and respectfully bow and walk away backwards in the presence of an elder or king. On the same day they could be attending a gathering of people supporting a political party.

Did you know?

People honour past leaders by visiting their **shrines** and leaving gifts and food.

King Letsie III of Lesotho (born 1963)

King Letsie III learned his kingdom's history and traditions from a young age. King Letsie's role is largely ceremonial but he is a modern king. He studied law at university and is involved with programmes to help young people, and to tackle the disease HIV/AIDS. Unlike some African kings, he has stated that he wants only one wife.

Nomads and pastoralists

The cultures of Africa's **nomadic** hunter-gatherers, fishermen, and **pastoralist** herders reflect their life of travel. They can cover long distances between hunting and fishing grounds and grazing lands according to the seasons. Some return at times to patches of settled farmland. Few true hunter-gatherer communities remain, but small groups of Hadza men in northern Tanzania still live by hunting animals, from baboons to buffalo. They collect honey by following the call of the honey-bird to beehives. Hadza women gather roots, shoots, leaves, berries, and fruits from native plants.

In the cooler season, the Hadza stop to build a shelter from branches and leaves, which they can complete in just an hour. After a good day's hunting, they tell stories of great hunting trips. Hunter-gatherers like the Hadza take only what they need from their environment.

Hadza use the boiled sap of the desert rose to poison the tips of their hunting arrows for a quick kill.

Moving with animals

Pastoralist herders are spread across the whole of Africa, from the Bedouin in the north, to the Himba in the south. They herd a mixture of camels, cattle, sheep, and goats. Livestock is eaten, traded, and used as a wedding gift to a bride's family.

Did you know?

The great baobab tree provides nomads with water stored in its trunk. The leaves are eaten and used as medicine. The fruits can be eaten, too. Baobab bark is made into rope and cloth.

Tuareg nomads travel on camels. Camels provide milk, cheese, meat, and skins.

CUSTOMS AND ACTIVITIES

Greeting people is never cut short in Africa. How you do it depends on whether you are male or female, your age, and your social position. Young people are often expected to bow or nod their heads to their elders. With each other, though, they use a lot of high fives! Men usually shake hands firmly. In some Muslim communities, men touch the chest over the heart to show they are truthful. In Morocco, they might briefly kiss each cheek. Men rarely shake hands with women unless they have a professional relationship.

A friendly handshake is very similar all over the world!

Greetings

People usually say "Hello" or "How are things?" without naming the person they are greeting. They might use a general term such as "Mr" or "Sister". After the first hello, it is important to take time to ask about the family's health. Then they may ask about work or a new car, or almost anything else, as long as it is not too personal.

When people visit someone's home they call out first and wait for an answer. Just banging on the door is impolite.

Did you know?

Here are three ways of shaking hands:

1. Shake the right hand normally. Then, without letting go, slip the hand around the other person's thumb. Shake the hand again.

2. Shake the hand. Then link and snap each other's middle finger. The louder the snap the better!

3. Shake the hand and move the arm wildly at the same time, like the Luhya people of Kenya.

Sharing fun

All over Africa, people get together for harvest or family celebrations. They also gather to take part in traditional games, sports, and pastimes. They follow Africa's favourite global sports, too: football, basketball, volleyball, wrestling, boxing, and athletics. Young children love to play tag. Games often start with players moving in a circle, with the chaser in the middle. When everyone's exhausted, they might take part in clapping or stick-tapping with singing or chanting. These are great playground pastimes. Marbles, a game played in Egypt since ancient times, is very popular.

This is *bao,* one of the world's most difficult board games. It began in East Africa.

Didier Drogba (born 1978)

Didier Drogba of Ivory Coast is one of Africa's many great footballers. He is a successful striker for Ivory Coast and for Chelsea Football Club in London. Didier set up his own charity to help health and education projects in Africa. He is also a Goodwill Ambassador for the United Nations Development Programme.

Fighting skills

Sport gets serious for young adults who want to pass into the next age grade. Some have to take part in wrestling or stick-fighting challenges. These are more like martial arts, with special moves and codes.

The Nuba of Sudan are skilled wrestlers, while the Xhosa and Zulu of southern Africa are famed for their stick-fighting. They use one or two sticks and sometimes shields. All these sports are watched keenly by spectators.

This Nuba wrestler has just defeated his opponent.

Culture around food

Across Africa, a meal is an important cultural event. Family and guests often sit around a huge shared platter on a floor mat or floor cloth, or at a table. People eat with their right hand, but cutlery is also widely used.

A feast of Africa

In Ethiopia, coffee is a traditional drink. It is served at breakfast with *injera* (flatbread) and *shiro wat* (chickpea stew). Over in West Africa, the Fulani start the day with *fura*, their cows' soured milk mixed with millet cereal.

This is a traditional north African market stall, piled with fruits, herbs, and chillies.

The main evening meal in north Africa could be slow-cooked lamb with herbs, saffron, spices, and pickled lemon.

In the south, it might be maize porridge mixed in a huge wooden **pestle and mortar** and served with a spicy bean and vegetable stew. Chicken is a feast for visitors and special occasions.

Some foods are believed to be unclean or even unlucky. In mid-western Nigeria, some believe that a warrior could weaken if he eats snails.

Many cooks use three-stone stoves heated with wood or charcoal. Bottled-gas or electric stoves are also used.

Agnes Mwang'ombe

Kenya's Agnes Mwang'ombe of the University of Nairobi is a scientist who studies plants. She knows that it is hard to grow food in dry parts of Africa, so she tries to develop new, tough crop varieties. She also supports training for women farmers. Over 60 per cent of African farmers are women.

RELIGIOUS BELIEFS AND PRACTICES

Religious beliefs are deep-rooted in everyday African culture. Creation beliefs are told as stories in many parts of Africa. They tell how a creator god brought people into the world and to their homeland.

In East Africa, the Kamba, Kikuyu, and Masai people believe in a creator god called Ngai. Traditionally, Masai believe that Ngai split a tree into three pieces, creating three men. The first was a Masai and Ngai gave him a stick to help herd his cattle. The second was a Kikuyu and Ngai gave him a hoe to dig the land. The third was a Kamba and Ngai gave him a bow and arrow for hunting.

Kikuyu people believe that the god Ngai rests on top of sacred Mount Kenya (shown here).

This is a ceremony to appoint a new *sangoma*, a South African shaman.

People believe their creator god is part of a huge spirit world. They believe that **ancestors** become spirits. A strangely shaped rock may be a spirit, too, or a huge tree, or even a whole forest. Spirits are thought to harm or heal, so people honour them by offering food, drink, and gifts at ancestors' shrines or near trees or rocks.

YOUNG PEOPLE

Imagine as a boy or girl that you are told you have a special gift that allows you to communicate with the spirit world. People say you should become a **shaman** when you are older. A shaman is believed to receive advice from spirits to help people. Today, some shamans also have other jobs, such as being doctors or teachers.

World faiths in Africa

Africa is next to the Middle East, where three major **world faiths** began: Judaism, Christianity, and Islam. Christianity and Islam each have about 450 million African followers. Many followers still respect their traditional spiritual **heritage**, too.

Judaism was the first world faith to come to Africa. The oldest community has been living on Djerba Island off Tunisia for nearly 2,500 years. Many Ethiopian Jews now live in Israel, but there are still baked-brick **synagogues** in northern Ethiopia.

On Sundays, you might see vast gatherings of African Christians singing joyful hymns of praise. Or you might see small numbers praying beneath neat church shelters in a forest clearing. Africa has also produced great Christian thinkers, such as Saint Augustine of Hippo (354–430 CE).

Five times a day, Muslims obey the call to prayer across north, west, and east Africa. Muslim children attend **mosques** after school, where they learn the **Qur'an**. Education is important in Islam. Africa produced great Islamic universities, such as Djenné and Timbuktu in West Africa.

Desmond Tutu (born 1931)

Desmond Tutu of South Africa is a great Christian thinker and archbishop. He grew up when South Africa was ruled by white people, who did not want blacks to share power. He preached justice for peoples of all backgrounds. In 1984, Archbishop Tutu received the international Nobel Peace Prize.

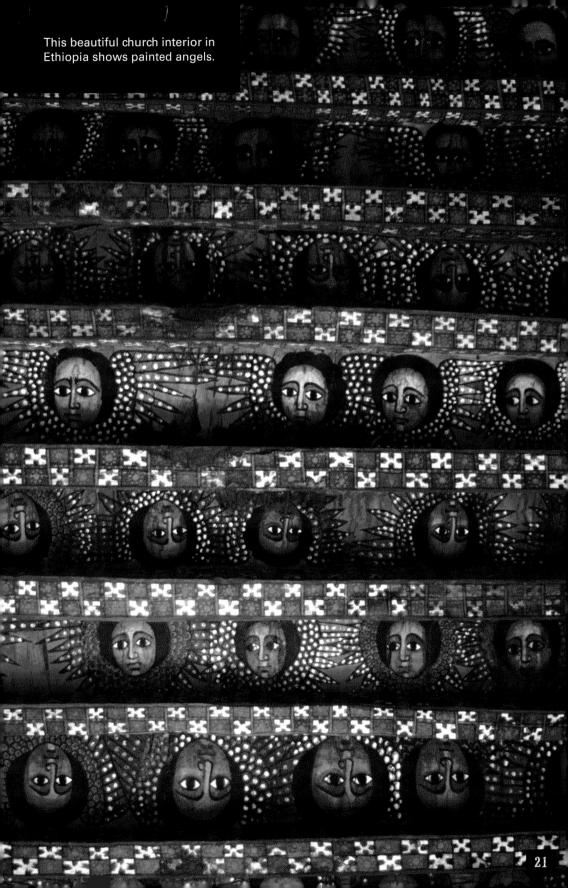

This beautiful church interior in Ethiopia shows painted angels.

21

Life ceremonies

Africa's thousands of life-stage traditions begin as soon as a baby is born. A bead, stone, or bone necklet is often hung around the baby's neck to protect against harmful spirits. After a while, a naming ceremony will take place.

Did you know?

At the naming ceremony, an Edo baby from West Africa is presented with honey, sugar, and bitter **kola nut** to represent the good and bad in life. The Chagga of East Africa name the baby only when the first tooth appears. In Islam, a name must be pleasant, peaceful, and not embarrassing!

Getting married

At a traditional hunter-gatherer wedding, the couple might simply take a fire stick from their separate fires and light a new one together. Elsewhere, there is plenty of fuss! A Masai bride's head is shaved and covered with animal fat to mark a new stage in her life. A Fulani bride chases away the groom's friends from his home before it becomes her own. The families of a Zulu bride and groom hold singing and dancing competitions.

When life ends

At the end of his or her life, a Muslim's body will be washed in scented water and shrouded in white cotton cloth. The Kalabari of the Niger Delta decorate the funeral bed and the mourners with colourful handmade cloth. Across much of Africa, the anniversary of a person's death is honoured by gifts to the spirits.

The Dogon of Mali wear *sirige* masks in the *dama* ceremony to honour the dead. The mask represents the family house of the person who died.

23

DECORATIVE ARTS

African art can be both spiritual and creative. Africa is famous for its stunning pottery, sculpture, jewellery, and fabrics. However, art often begins with the body.

Body painting

Body art can show identity and position in society, especially for teenagers and young adults. It is also a fashion statement! Make-up can be mixed from crushed minerals such as chalk, or from ground charcoal. Kohl eyeliner is made from oils, ashes, and minerals and is used across northern Africa. Dried henna-leaf ink makes fine patterns on the hands and feet.

Every day, Ethiopia's Surma children are made up with different chalk patterns.

YOUNG PEOPLE

Ga'anda girls of northern Nigeria and Chad have unique body markings. From the age of five their skin is patterned with tiny lines of small cuts. As the cuts heal, the skin is raised, making beautiful designs. The cuts are added to every year, but end when a young woman is ready for marriage.

More than masks

Masks are worn in drama, dance, and ceremony across Africa south of the Sahara. They can represent the spirits of ancestors and nature. Masks can look quite scary but they are often worn to protect against bad spirits and to bring wealth and good harvests.

Mask-makers use wood, bark, cloth, **raffia**, basketware, and metal. Masks can be painted, and decorated with feathers, shells, and beads. Some are handheld while others cover the head right down to the shoulders.

This Nigerian artist is carving an elaborate mask out of wood.

Fashion in Africa

In modern African cities there is both international fashion and local style. In traditional areas, clothes and accessories can show people's clan and life stage. They can reveal if people are married, are a senior wife, or show if they are not quite ready to settle down yet.

Tailors make bright patterned cloth into tunics, trousers, shawls, and wraps. Patterns and colours change with fashion. *Nwentoma* cloth from Ghana is also known as *kente*, or "basket" cloth, because the patterns look like basket-weaving.

Did you know?

Natural cloth dyes are made from plants and minerals. For example, reds come from all parts of the African madder plant. Deep blues are made from the leaves of indigo plants, while yellows and browns are taken from rocks and clays.

Cotton cloth is dyed a deep indigo blue in Kano City's ancient dye pits in northern Nigeria.

Fikirte Addis (born 1981)

Fikirte Addis is an Ethiopian designer who uses fine local cloth and traditional motifs to create modern styles. In 2011, Fikirte won the "Origin Africa – Fibre to Fashion" competition for her designs. Her prize was a place at New York's Africa Fashion Week 2011. Fikirte also campaigns against child labour in fashion.

Jewellery

Jewellery style is varied, from the delicate silver **filigree** of north Africa to the fine beadwork of east and southern Africa. Cowry-shell necklaces on the West African coast and copper-coloured cornelian stone beads of the Fulani to the north show huge contrasts in style and materials.

This woman's fine white beaded necklace shows that she belongs to Kisingo, the largest Masai clan.

Interior design

Traditional African rugs, floor mats, and furniture are beautiful, practical, and use local materials. The patterns on them identify which group of people made them.

Did you know?

Some special plant species used for craftwork and furniture include:

- Acacia tree bark for Nama hunter-gatherers' matting homes.
- Acacia tree wood fibres for particle board in Tunisia.
- The small mignonette tree, for strong basketware and henna dye.
- Coconut husk fibres for matting and mattress stuffing.

The rugs in this Berber tent help to keep it warm on chilly desert nights.

A wealth of materials

The rugs and wall hangings used by nomads are rolled up every time the community moves camp, so the fabrics have to be strong. Rugs made by Bedouin and Tuareg nomads are often a mixture of animal hair and cotton. These Muslim nomads are forbidden by their faith to make images of people. Instead, they use bold geometric patterns, coloured by natural dyes. Coconut mattresses lie on top of grand Swahili high-beds made from African hardwoods. In West Africa, Akan kings sit on ornate carved hardwood stools, a symbol of their power.

You may not think it to look at them, but these are coffins made in Ghana!

Furniture for the afterlife is important to the Ga of Ghana. For 60 years they have built coffins to suit the character, status, or profession of people who have died. A coffin could be in the shape of a taxi, aeroplane, bird, book, or even a mobile phone! Ga coffins have become so popular that you can now order them online.

Architectural detail

The massive stone walls of Great Zimbabwe, a trading city, were built over 1,000 years ago in East Africa. They contrast with the neat, lightweight woven homes of hunter-gatherers and the multistorey clay grain stores of farmers. Even modern concrete flats have a unique African style.

Southern Africa's Basotho and Ndebele communities paint bold plasterwork designs. These are to encourage a good harvest and plenty of rainfall.

Powerful architecture

Traditional rulers' palaces can boast dramatic structures and details. You might see high thatched roofs that sweep down almost to the ground, or tall, decorated brick towers, called turrets, built into thick walls. Palaces of West African *emirs* are covered in brightly painted plasterwork with raised plaster shapes, such as flowers. On the East African coast, the grand multistorey mansions of Swahili trading families are protected by massive hardwood doors covered with ornate carving. Across Africa, plasterwork on homes and grain stores is often decorated with grooved patterns in waves or swirls.

Diébéde Francis Kéré (born 1965)

Diébéde Francis Kéré is from Burkina Faso in West Africa. He was once a carpenter and is now an exciting new architect. Diébéde uses local materials and the skills of local people to make attractive buildings that suit hot climates. Their details include roofs that allow air to circulate above dome-shaped ceilings. Cool courtyards separate rooms, and sliding shutters control air flow.

Mali's grand Djenné Mosque is the world's largest sun-baked brick structure. Turrets are capped with removable air vents and ostrich eggs sit on top as symbols of purity.

PERFORMANCE

Performance in Africa often combines drama, drumming, and song. It can celebrate life events, history and ancestors, or simply tell a really good story.

Learning through stories

Storytelling and spoken history are age-old traditions. Stories teach children about social rules and life's challenges. African animal stories often show how sometimes we have to do difficult things in order to survive. Ijapa the tortoise and Anansi the tricksy spider play out their mischief in West Africa. Sungura the Hare stars in cunning tales from east, central, and southern Africa. Drums, tapped sticks, and clapping accompany the most exciting or scary moments.

While many stories are passed down by word of mouth, Africa also has a long tradition of writing. Mali's Timbuktu library holds 700,000 ancient manuscripts.

Speaking and singing history

Creation stories give people a sense of their own identity and place. So do past events, which in West Africa are told by families of historians called *griots*. *Griots* tell, chant, or sing rulers' deeds, often going back hundreds of years.

Sona Maya Jobarteh (born 1983)

Sona Maya Jobarteh is the first woman *kora* (stringed instrument) *griot*. She comes from one of the five most famous *griot* families. Sona performs traditional songs but creates modern compositions for the *kora*, too. She sometimes performs with guitarists and other musicians.

Dance and drama

Dance is a celebration of life and work. It can also be very dramatic. Masked dancers often act out the spirits of nature and ancestors to honour their power and to please them.

YOUNG PEOPLE

In central Africa, Chokwe boys aged 8–12 stay in a *mukanda* camp, away from home. In camp, they learn how to become men. It is a very tough time for them. Masked dancers represent ancestors who protect the boys during their difficult stay. In a different dance, a masked man acts out the part of Pwo, who shows boys how to recognize skill, grace, and charm in a girl.

Dance steps can be complicated, with different rhythms for feet, body, head, and arms. Even accompanying drums can have a different rhythm. Dancers often have to carry props. Women from Birnin Kebbi in Nigeria perform a fisherman's dance. Each dancer moves with a billowing cloth in their hands to represent a fishing-net.

Many dancers include modern steps and styles such as breakdance and hip-hop. Dance troupes entertain crowds at festivals and at their countries' annual Independence Day celebrations. They entertain people in theatres all around the world. Inner-city dance troupes, such as Kibera in Nairobi, use traditional moves to act out important issues in people's lives. Some dancers take health messages to remote areas.

These children are performing the South African mine dance. This dance uses traditional moves to show the difficult lives of miners in gold and coal mines.

Drums and drumming

Drums give rhythm and strength to dance, drama, and song. They can greet visitors, honour spirits, and celebrate happy occasions. Sometimes drumbeats take on the part of a character.

Drums can symbolize power. On official occasions, a 15-drum ensemble (group of musicians) greets the King of Baganda in Uganda. Each of these *entenga* drums is tuned to a different note. In Ghana, the Akan *etwie* drum makes a sound like a leopard's snarl. It is a symbol of the Akan king's power. The snarl is made by scraping powder across the drum skin with a drumstick.

Did you know?

Drums can be made from ceramic pots, **gourds**, hollowed-out wood, and oil drums. The drum skins are usually made from the skins of goats or antelope. Drums can have different shapes, such as a barrel, hourglass, or a frame, like a tambourine. For extra sounds, pieces of metal or small bells can be attached. Soft wax patches are stuck to the skin to make a different note.

These are traditional bongo drums.

Mamady Keita (born 1950)

Mamady Keita of Guinea is an international Grandmaster of the huge Malinke *djembe* drum. Mamady was meant to be a master hunter and healer like his father, but a shaman told Mamady's mother to let him follow his dreams and talents. Young Mamady drummed all day on upturned cooking pots. His mother took notice and the rest is history.

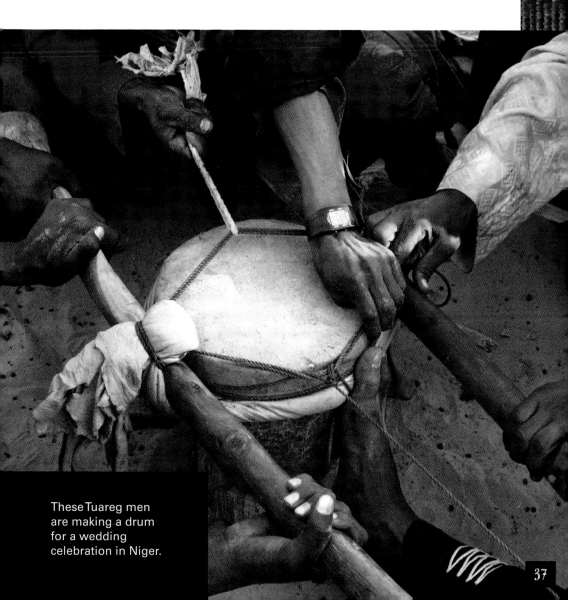

These Tuareg men are making a drum for a wedding celebration in Niger.

Salif Keita (born 1949)

Salif Keita is a world famous singer-songwriter from Mali. He was born into a royal family. Salif's family rejected his love of music but by the 1970s he and his group were stars. They play *balafon*, *kora*, guitar, *djembe* drum, saxophone, and keyboard to produce a unique sound.

Music and musical instruments

Across Africa, traditional musicians praise kings and courtiers. They honour spirits and mark life's celebrations. In towns and cities, top hip-hop bands entertain the young. However, music really belongs to everybody. There are songs for ploughing and harvesting and for pounding **yams** or grain. There are lullabies and singing-rhymes for children's games. Everyone can join in.

Baaba Maal is a famous musician from Senegal. He blends traditional, jazz, South American, and electronic styles.

Musicians play a huge variety of instruments, from north Africa's lutes and reed instruments to the *mbira* thumb pianos of the south. Round or bell-shaped gongs, wooden clappers, xylophones, rattles, whistles, and flutes are played across Africa.

Southern Africa's Shona people play the *mbira* to bring out ancestor spirits. The *mbira* sounds like rhythmic echoing chimes.

Did you know?

Gongs were once all made from bronze or iron. Oil drums and metal roof sheeting are now also used. Dried gourds make natural rattles. The seeds inside shake around like beads. Gourds can also be made into stringed instruments, such as the *kora*. *Balafon* and other xylophone types are made from Africa's hardwoods, while flutes can be made of bamboo, wood, plant roots, or animal horns.

AFRICAN CULTURE IN THE 21ST CENTURY

Africa's peoples have cultures that go back hundreds and sometimes thousands of years. However, culture never stays the same in any society. This is especially true when people move to cities for work and a new life. Here, new cultures are born. Through modern communications, global culture is a part of African life. In turn, African ideas, poetry, novels, art, crafts, and music are enjoyed throughout the world.

A culture of science and technology

Africa responds to problems in a way that suits Africa's culture. New crop varieties that grow in dry climates have been developed. Tree-planting and water conservation projects are helping to slow the effects of climate change, which is drying up the land. Solar-powered stoves stop trees and shrubs from being used as fuel.

YOUNG PEOPLE

Some Africans believe that modern life is affecting old values of respect, duty, and helpfulness. So, at school, pupils are expected to sweep and tidy the classroom and grounds or work on the school allotment. Social Studies is a key subject in many countries, teaching responsibilities as well as rights.

Mobile-phone banking such as Kenya's M-Pesa service is helping to develop businesses. It is also allowing city workers to send money back to their families in rural towns and villages. There, communities use it for education and to build a better life.

These children live in Djibouti City, the capital of Djibouti.

41

TIMELINE

BCE

500,000   The world's first modern humans evolve in Africa

8,000   Communities develop on Egypt's Nile Delta

CE

50–100   Christianity comes to Africa

100   Camels are introduced into north Africa, allowing trade across the Sahara Desert

100–200   East Africa trades with people throughout the Mediterranean region and Asia

670s onwards   Islam comes to Africa, and influences architecture, art, and writing

800   Swahili culture develops on the east coast of the continent and in island trading ports

1000   The Great Zimbabwe stone settlement is built

1240   Djenné Mosque is built in Mali

1492   Christopher Columbus reaches the Americas. The trade in African slaves begins, taking African culture to the Americas.

1500s onwards   Crops and goods from the Americas and Europe enter Africa

1800s   Missionaries from the United States and Europe spread Christianity throughout sub-Saharan Africa

1800s–1900s   European countries colonize and divide up Africa

1940s–1950s   Writers, poets, film makers, sculptors, and artists create works that criticize their colonial rulers

1950s   African musicians blend traditional music with jazz and South American styles, especially in the Congo and West Africa

1960s   Most African countries achieve independence from their colonial rulers

1960s–2000s   Modern African culture bursts on to the world stage with film makers such as Ousmane Sembene and artists such as Viye Diba

CULTURAL MAP

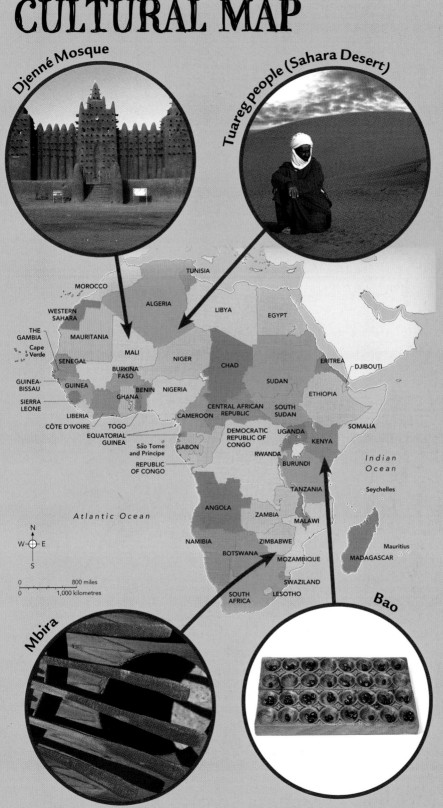

Djenné Mosque

Tuareg people (Sahara Desert)

MOROCCO
TUNISIA
WESTERN SAHARA
ALGERIA
LIBYA
EGYPT
THE GAMBIA
MAURITANIA
Cape Verde
SENEGAL
MALI
NIGER
ERITREA
DJIBOUTI
BURKINA FASO
CHAD
SUDAN
GUINEA-BISSAU
GUINEA
BENIN
NIGERIA
SIERRA LEONE
GHANA
CENTRAL AFRICAN REPUBLIC
ETHIOPIA
LIBERIA
CÔTE D'IVOIRE
TOGO
CAMEROON
SOUTH SUDAN
SOMALIA
EQUATORIAL GUINEA
DEMOCRATIC REPUBLIC OF CONGO
UGANDA
São Tomé and Principe
GABON
KENYA
REPUBLIC OF CONGO
RWANDA
BURUNDI
Indian Ocean
TANZANIA
Seychelles
Atlantic Ocean
ANGOLA
ZAMBIA
MALAWI
N
W—E
S
NAMIBIA
ZIMBABWE
MADAGASCAR
Mauritius
BOTSWANA
MOZAMBIQUE
0   800 miles
0   1,000 kilometres
SOUTH AFRICA
LESOTHO
SWAZILAND

Mbira

Bao

GLOSSARY

age grade stage of life with its own rules, through which a person passes to get to the next stage

age set group of men or women who pass through life stages together rather than as individuals

ancestor family relation from a very long time ago, such as a great-great-grandparent

clan group of families or villages that share a common culture

creation story story that describes how a people were created, how the world began, and how they came into it

culture customs, social organisation, and achievements of a particular nation, people, or group

elder senior member of a family or clan

emir Muslim ruler

filigree delicate lacy patterns

gourd large dried-out seed pod used for making musical instruments, bowls, and spoons

heritage anything from the past handed down by tradition

homestead farmhouse and its outbuildings

kinship family ties and sense of belonging

kola nut tropical forest nut that helps keep you awake when you chew it

mosque building in which Muslims meet and worship

mukanda camp set up away from villages and towns where boys go through ceremonies to become men

nomadic moving from one place to another for much of the year

pastoralist farmer who herds cattle, sheep, goats, and camels from one grazing land to another

pestle and mortar thick stick with a rounded end (pestle) that pounds or mixes food in a sturdy wooden or stone bowl (mortar)

Qur'an holy book of the Muslims

raffia strong fibres made from different varieties of palm leaf

shaman person with a gift for contacting the spirit world

shanty town makeshift homes put up at the edges of towns and cities by people looking for work

shrine building or small structure that is devoted to a religion

sirige tall mask worn at a ceremony for the dead carried out by the Dogon people in West Africa

symbol sign

synagogue Jewish place of worship

tradition customs that are passed on from one generation to the next

wattle material for making fences and walls, consisting of rods woven with twigs and branches

world faith religion that has spread across the world and has many followers

yam root of a climbing vine found in tropical countries

FIND OUT MORE

Books

African Myths (Graphic Myths), Gary Jeffrey (Book House, 2006)
An Illustrated Atlas of Africa (Continents in Close-up)
    Malcolm Porter (Cherrytree Books, 2007)
Letters to Africa (UCLan Publishing, 2010)

Websites

www.schoolnet.na/games/map/africa.html
This is a jigsaw puzzle quiz that helps you learn the countries of Africa. There are several levels. The hardest one really is hard!

https://www.cia.gov/library/publications/the-world-factbook/index.html
Find up-to-the-minute facts about all the African countries on this website.

CDs

Djembe and African Drums (Playasound, 2000)
This CD has drumming and *balafon* playing. Listen out for the sounds of tapped sticks, rattles, and flutes in the background.

Zimbabwe: Shona Mbira Music (Nonesuch, 1971-1974, re-released 2002)
You can hear haunting *mbira* notes and the buzz of rattles, with some singing.

Golden Voice: the Best of Salif Keita (Wrasse Records, 2001)
You can hear drums, *balafon*, *kora*, guitar, rattle, and many other sounds, including South American influences.

Places to visit

The British Museum, London

www.britishmuseum.org

Visit the British Museum to see African cultural objects, from pottery and bronze sculptures to masks and carvings.

African culture workshops

www.timeout.com/london/kids/features/4818/Best_African_culture_for_kids_in_London.html

Visit this website to find workshops in London on African textiles, jewellery, drumming, printing, and dance.

Horniman Museum, London

www.horniman.ac.uk

The Horniman Museum contains many ceremonial and spiritual African objects.

International Slavery Museum, Liverpool

www.liverpoolmuseums.org.uk/ism/

The museum shows how and why Africans were captured and sent to the Americas. It also shows the culture that they took with them.

More topics to research

What topic did you like reading about most in this book? Did you find out anything that you thought was particularly interesting? Choose a topic that you liked, such as food, buildings, or religion, and try to find out more about it. You could visit one of the places mentioned above, have a look at one of the websites, or visit your local library to do some research. You could also try some things out for yourself, such as listening to some African music, making a Dogon mask, or shaking hands with your friends African-style!

INDEX